An Inspiring Comeba

THE MILLIONAIRE WITHIN

Reinvent Yourself for Success and
Unleash **THE MILLIONAIRE WITHIN** You

Paul Noor

Contents

Acknowledgments

- Dr. Breitenfeldt, the founder of the stuttering workshop at Eastern Washington University in Cheney, Washington. He gave me all the inspiration and tools that I needed to overcome my speech disorder.
- Toastmasters Clubs, which created a positive and supportive environment for me to work on my public speaking skills and allowed me to fall down as many times as needed until I gained confidence.
- Hank Stone, a professional actor, writer, director, speech coach, and a friend, who tirelessly trained me and brought out the best in me.

Introduction

I started my engineering and construction business from zero. No one rolled out the red carpet for me. After more than twenty years of hard work and sending two sons to college, for the first time I became a self-made millionaire. While I was at the very peak of my home building business and about to semi-retire, I became entangled in an unfortunate and destructive divorce. I tried my hardest to finish it in a friendly manner so that I could save my business. Unfortunately, that did not happen.

After two and a half years of court battles, I lost my house, and later, my business. Most of my savings and retirement money went toward the expensive legal fees, as well. In the end, it was so bad that although I voluntarily gave her half of the assets, it felt as if the two divorce attorneys got the other half. On top of that, because of my previously high income in the home-building business, I had to pay her a huge monthly alimony—until she remarried. Since my only way out was for her to get remarried, I was praying and begging everyone, "Please Marry My Wife."

At about the same time, the housing market in central California where I was working started to collapse. I could not even pay my own bills. How could I pay the unrealistic monthly alimony? Everything seemed to cave in at the same time. In a short span, I went from Hero to Zero. The destruction was brutal. A homebuilder became homeless.

Since there was no way that I could earn enough money to pay the alimony, I decided to leave the country. I found a job as an English teacher in China that would pay me about $800 per month, and that was enough to live over there. Although English is my second language, to the Chinese I was speaking English like a Harvard graduate. They couldn't hear a difference.

Despite everything, I was very concerned about her. She was my first love, and we were married for 29 years. How was she going to take care of herself?

On the other hand, I had to question why should I care for her? I had tried my hardest to finish it in a friendly manner, and she refused. I voluntarily gave her our beautiful five-bedroom family house that was paid off, her Mercedes Benz that was paid off, all of the furniture that was paid off, and a lump sum of cash. She had a master's degree and children in college. She could have easily supported herself. I should not have felt bad at all for not being able to take care of her. It was time for me to leave her and take care of my own life before I lost more. It was time for me to move to China. Let her suffer her life without me. It would be a BIG punishment for her.

About a month after our divorce while I was preparing to move to China, one of my friends called me and said, "I have news about your ex-wife."

I angrily said, "I don't care anymore. I've had enough…but…what is the news?"

He said, "Your ex-wife is getting married to your neighbor."

I screamed, "Whaaaaat! She kept me in court for two and a half years, ruined my construction business, and now she is getting married to my neighbor." How naive I was!

A few minutes later, I realized that this was actually great news. With her getting remarried so quickly, I wouldn't have to pay alimony much longer. I believed I had just struck a gold mine. Suddenly, my neighbor had become an angel sent from heaven to save me.

Now, I had another challenge: Will their marriage go according to plan? How soon will they get married? What can I do to make sure that their marriage will go smoothly?

There were too many unknowns and uncertainties. Time was working against me. I was out of work, and I had to put my plan for moving to China on hold—at least temporarily. I was just waiting, and waiting, and waiting. I could hear the clock ticking. I had never been so vulnerable. My whole life depended on their marriage. If they got married, I could stay in the United States and restart my life. If, God forbid, their marriage plan failed, I would have to move to China and teach the English language. With English being my second language, I could have ruined the Chinese people's English skills for years to come. It was one of those crucial times in my life, and I just had to wait and pray that their marriage would go according to plan.

Soon after, a friend called and said that he had received a wedding invitation. He said that the wedding date was about a month later. This news was like music to my ears. It was like rain in the desert. How could I get so lucky? At the same time, the tension inside of me was building up. That one month felt like an eternity. It wasn't just her wedding; it was my BIG DAY too—I would soon have my freedom back.

A week before the wedding, I even left town to make sure that I wouldn't disturb their plans. The wedding was on a Saturday night, and I went to Las Vegas to celebrate my freedom. I was with a friend, and we spent the evening walking up and down the street, and keeping me occupied. I was anxiously waiting for the good news: the confirmation of the marriage. I waited, and waited, and waited—but there was no news and no phone calls. It was devastating. I barely slept that night. When I did, I had a scary dream that the wedding had been cancelled and I was teaching English in a village in China. After school, she and her attorney chased me down a narrow alley behind the building with a big syringe and a long needle to suck the last drop of blood from my body. I ran, and ran, and ran. I ran as fast as I could. Luckily, I fell off a tall bridge. My head smashed into a big rock and I woke up. What a relief! It was morning.

I packed up my stuff and headed toward Los Angeles to see my parents. Still no news. Finally, at about ten in the morning, while I was driving across the desert, I called one of our mutual friends who had attended the wedding. I asked him about it. He said, "Paul, congratulations! The wedding went smoothly. You are off the hook."

I pulled my car over and parked it on the side of the road. I got out and walked to the middle of the barren land and screamed: Yes! Yes! Yes! Thank you! Thank you! Thank you! I then screamed even more, as hard as I could, to make sure it would reach the heavens. It felt as if the outgoing husband was happier than the incoming husband.

Her surprise and quick marriage to our neighbor was a real blessing. It happened four months after our divorce. I couldn't be happier, and I got my freedom back.

CHASING MY DREAM

Unfortunately, after our divorce, the housing market crashed, and I was out of work. But I was determined to get back on my feet and reinvent myself for success. How could I reinvent myself? How could I even get back on my feet? At my low point, I had lost practically everything. Everything, except: THE MILLIONAIRE WITHIN me.

When I was in the construction business I had learned Cardinal Rules of Success that made me a self-made millionaire. When everything fell apart in my life, I decided to restart my journey by using those Cardinal Rules.

I then decided to write this book and help others unleash THE MILLIONAIRE WITHIN them, and to speak at different organizations so that I could share what I had learned with as many people as I could, but I had a major obstacle in front of me: I could not speak in front of people. I had a severe stuttering problem.

I have been struggling with my stuttering since I was about three years old. I remember that when I was in high school my stuttering got so out of control that finishing a simple sentence was a major challenge, but I didn't lose hope. I finished high school and then attended college and earned a bachelor's degree and a master's degree in civil engineering. Since my goal was to become a college professor, I entered a PhD program. I was hoping that while I worked toward my PhD, I would find a cure for my stuttering so I could teach at a university.

Unfortunately, at that time my stuttering became so severe that learning sign language seemed to be the best option for me to communicate, and my dream of becoming a college professor was completely shattered. Obviously, no university would hire me to teach. With my severe stuttering at that time, I would have kept the whole class stuck on the first chapter of the book.

I started my new journey "From Stuttering to Public Speaking" with many unknowns. I knew it would be a rough path because I had traveled it before. Unfortunately, I had failed in the past. This time I was motivated more than ever before. This time I was unstoppable. This time I was determined to take advantage of the new changes in my life, and to make something better of myself. This time I had a message to share with people, and I had to speak in front of audiences—to do that, I had to overcome my stuttering. This time I knew that I had to pick up the pieces and climb a steep wall. I also knew that if I didn't take action immediately, I would run out of steam quickly. So, with every ounce of energy in me…I decided to reinvent my life for success, starting with a blank canvas.

I am proud to say that, as I am writing this book, I am living my dream life as a keynote speaker and corporate trainer. I have spoken at numerous places including Fortune 500 companies, and I am helping individuals and organizations to reinvent themselves for success.

If you think about it, crisis can actually be a good motivator. It is amazing how creative we become when we see that our very survival is in danger. Eventually, from the ashes of my former life rose a new career and a brighter future. In this book, I will teach you how to crush the obstacles on your path and reinvent yourself for success—even if you see no light at the end of the tunnel.

Those who knew me in the past and saw my severe stuttering believe that this is a miracle. How could this miracle have happened? I believe I am living my dream life because I was determined to take advantage of new changes in my life, and turn my failures into success. In doing that, I used the Five Cardinal Rules of Success that I had learned in my construction business. They are so crucial that I call them Cardinal Rules.

Always remember that life has so many ups and downs. Sometimes you have to close an old chapter and start a new one. When that happens, you have two options: either to put your failures, setbacks, and all those painful memories right in front of you like a wall and let it stop you from moving forward, or to use these Five Cardinal Rules to reinvent yourself for success. I strongly recommend the second option—because you deserve to be successful. In this book, you will learn them in detail.

Well, are you excited to learn these Five Cardinal Rules? Are you ready to unleash THE MILLIONAIRE WITHIN you? Then flip to the next page, and let's travel together to your better future…a much better future.

Paul
PaulNoor.com

Revised: April 21, 2017

Cardinal Rule #1:

Dump Your Trash

Before writing this book, I came up with five options for the title of the Cardinal Rule #1:

Love Your Enemy
Forgive Your Enemy
Let Go of Your Past
Dump Your Past
Dump Your Trash

My very favorite and number one choice has always been "Love Your Enemy." A good example of someone who put this philosophy into practice is Nelson Mandela. When he was released after twenty-seven years in prison, he immediately forgave the people who had put him there. When he became president of South Africa, he even invited his prison guards, who had kept him in captivity for so many years, to his inauguration ceremony. I am sure this is one of the reasons he is so admired in every corner of the world.

"Love Your Enemy" is a very powerful dictum, and it has always given me inspiration. It cleanses the heart and soul. It is like being born again, completely free from the past. To me, loving your enemy is the highest level of spirituality.

Even though "Love Your Enemy" is my favorite, unfortunately I didn't think it would be appropriate for the title of Cardinal Rule #1. Instead I chose "Dump Your Trash."

There are two reasons for that. The first is that this book is about the Five Cardinal Rules that I had learned in my construction business that helped me to thrive in business and in life. In the construction business, we don't love our trash. We dump our trash, and we dump it on a daily basis. I believe it is a great lesson that we all have to practice in life.

The second reason is that "Dump Your Trash" goes very well with what happened to me. Let's be honest, do you know anyone who loves his or her ex? I don't! You may like or respect your ex, but loving him or her is going too far. So, I decided to go with the more realistic title for Cardinal Rule #1: "Dump Your Trash."

If I had wanted to write a different book, I definitely would have used "Love Your Enemy." I just love that title—but not for this book. I leave it up to you to choose "Dump Your Trash," "Love Your Enemy," or even "Love Your Enemy and then Dump Them"—whatever makes you happy. Whatever is closest to your heart and spirit. Whatever gives you peace and freedom. But, regardless of your choice, make sure at the end to "Dump Your Trash" because that is what we are going to talk about in this chapter. After reading it, you will know exactly what I mean.

A GREAT LESSON
FROM MY CONSTRUCTION BUSINESS

I was in the construction business for over twenty years, and I would like to share with you a great lesson that I learned. The lesson is this: construction workers dump their trash before climbing up a ladder. In all those years, I never saw —not even once—a worker climb up a ladder while carrying trash. It would be very hard, it would waste their energy, and it would slow them down...so no one does it. Wow! If you think about it, there is a great lesson in there. It is so powerful!

The same thing is true in life. It will be very hard to move up the ladder in your life while carrying the trash from your past. First you have to dump it, and then you move up the ladder—as simple as that. If you don't believe me, next time you pass a construction site, stop and watch the workers climbing up the ladders. You will see what I am talking about. So the lesson is: Dump Your Trash first, and then move up the ladder in your life, wherever that ladder leads.

A GREAT LESSON
FROM MY TRIP TO JAPAN

Several years ago, I traveled to Asia. I took a suitcase and a backpack. One of my stops was in Tokyo, Japan. It was my first trip to that country. That city is crowded. It was overwhelming.

After sleeping in a local hotel in downtown Tokyo, I woke up early in the morning, took a shower, and ate my breakfast. I took my backpack and suitcase, and checked out of my hotel, intending to do some sightseeing. I got a map of the city and went to the underground train station. Wow! It was huge! Too many people were getting in and out of the trains. Getting into the train was so hard that they had someone standing by the door, pushing people in. And there I was with my suitcase and backpack trying to get into the train and go sightseeing. It was impossible!

At that moment, I came to the conclusion that, if I wanted to travel around, travel far, and see as many places as possible, I would have to get rid of my suitcase. I decided to leave it behind in that underground train station. So, in the middle of the station, I opened my suitcase, took out a few items that were important to me and put them in my backpack.

I didn't want to just leave the suitcase in the middle of the crowd. First, it wasn't right, and second, they could see me on the security camera and arrest me, so I took it to the security man who was nearby. He could hardly speak a few words of English. To make sure that he understood me clearly, I spoke at his level of broken English and said, "Me Not Need This Luggage. Trash… Trash…" He was confused and a little shocked by what I had said. To make sure that there was no confusion, I repeated again, "Me Not Need This Luggage. Trash…Trash…" I then gave my suitcase to him, so that he could dump it for me or give it to a homeless person.

I put my backpack on my back, pushed myself through the door of the train, and started my journey. It was a fun trip. I had a great time, and I was able to travel far and see a lot, only because I had dumped my luggage—or I better say, because I had dumped my trash.

If you want to travel far in your life, you must dump your trash, too. If you keep thinking about your past life, with all its failures, setbacks, and painful memories, you won't get very far. Carrying too many bags from the past will be very heavy, and it will slow you down. If you want to move forward, first you must Dump Your Trash.

DUMP YOUR TRASH FIRST SO YOU CAN REINVENT YOURSELF

In my case, it wasn't a matter of choice to dump my trash. I had to do it so I could be free and move forward. I set a new and ambitious goal to go "From Stuttering to Public Speaking"—something I had tried all my life and failed at many times. I had a rough journey ahead of me. I had a steep wall to climb. I couldn't afford to carry any trash with me. I had to dump all of it before starting my journey— and I did.

Some of my friends thought my goal was so out of reach that they laughed at me. They said, "You and public speaking? You will never reach that." They laughed at me very loudly. Not on the outside, but I could hear them laughing on the inside. While everybody saw me at the bottom of the barrel, I saw a brighter future in a new territory, far on the horizon. So I dumped all of my trash, and I started my long journey.

This time I was determined to complete the journey. I stayed away from anyone who doubted my faith or my ability to succeed. I knew that it would be a long journey over rugged terrain, full of surprises and unexpected obstacles. I had to travel far with limited supplies. The trip to Japan taught me a good lesson; that if I wanted to travel far, I had to dump my trash. Even just an extra ounce of it would consume the limited and precious fuel that I was carrying within me. I was over fifty years old; I had lost everything—the house that I had already paid off, the business that I had built up over twenty years, and most of my retirement money to two divorce attorneys. I couldn't gamble anymore. I didn't have many resources or much fuel left. I had no choice but to dump all of my trash, so that I could travel very light to an exciting future that was pulling me toward it like a magnet.

As I mentioned earlier, just two years after I started my new journey, I was the keynote speaker at a convention in California. Since then, I have spoken at numerous organizations including Fortune 500 companies. All of that occurred because, first, I dumped my trash.

I COULD NOT BELIEVE THIS MAN

One day at a social gathering, I met a man who told everyone that his first marriage had ended with a destructive divorce. He was talking about it to the people around him as if we were anxious to hear his story. The interesting part was that he had gotten married after that—not once but three times. Now he was with his fourth wife.

He said how much he hated his first ex-wife, although his divorce had happened many years ago. His story amazed me. While he was having fun with his wives, his first ex-wife took care of the kids by herself, and he still hated her. I couldn't stand sitting next him. I got up and moved across the room, as far away from him as I could. He definitely was carrying lots of trash from his past, and I definitely didn't want to be close to him or his trash.

21

MY ONE YEAR RULE
FOR DUMPING TRASH

I have a one-year rule in my life for dumping the trash in my house. I walk around, and if I see something that I haven't used in one year, I get rid of it. I do the same thing with my clothes. If I don't wear something for one year, I give it to the needy (except in the case of special clothing for occasional wear).

If you want to buy new clothes, you have to get rid of some clothes that you have not been wearing. You have to make room in your closet for your new clothes. If you want to meet the love of your life, you have to dump the memory of the person you had been dating in the past. You have to make room for a new person to come into your life.

HOW TO DUMP YOUR TRASH

As I mentioned earlier, you have to Dump Your Trash first, and then move up the ladder in your life —as simple as that. Some of you may say, "Paul, that is easier said than done. It is impossible for me to dump my trash. I have been in a destructive relationship. I have been living in a trashy environment for many years. It seems as if the trash got stuck to me with super glue. It is impossible to get rid of all those failures, setbacks, and painful memories. It is like my life is nothing but a pile of trash." Well, I truly understand it, because I had experienced it. Luckily, I found a few great techniques for dumping the trash from my past. I am using them, and I already feel great. Let me explain.

As I was eagerly looking for a solution to my dilemma, once again I found the answer in my construction business. I found it in a dirty bucket that I was washing my construction truck with. Yes, I found the answer in that dirty bucket.

One day as I was washing my truck, the telephone rang. It was a friend of mine. I was expecting it to be a short conversation. I got lazy and I did not turn off the water. Instead, I put the end of the water hose in the bucket while the water was running, then I answered the phone.

When I started talking, I completely forgot about the rest of the world—let alone the running water in the bucket. Suddenly I remembered it, and I rushed outside to turn it off. But instead, I saw something quite interesting. It really caught my attention.

Before I took the call, the bucket was full of soapy and dirty water. When I came back after that long telephone call, the water in the bucket was practically clean. As the fresh water was running to the bottom of the bucket, the soapy and dirty water was overflowing from the top. The more fresh water that went to the bottom of the bucket, the more dirty water that came out from the top. Very soon the fresh water had replaced the dirty water. And that gave me the answer I had been looking for— how to dump my trash from my past.

I realized that the same simple process can work with our brains, too. We need to pour positive material into our brains, so the negative and painful memories will overflow from the top. And we should do it every day.

My recommendations:

1— Monitor the thoughts that enter your brain. Experts believe that every day more than fifty thousand thoughts go through our brains. Unfortunately, some of them are negative and unhealthy. When it comes to our food, some people are so health conscious that they watch every little thing they eat, but when it comes to their mental health, they just leave the gate wide open. Everything can go through.

2— Read at least one positive, motivational, and inspirational book per month. If you read only thirty minutes every night before going to sleep, you should be able to read one book per month.

3— Every morning, before you start your day, say positive words, and say them loudly. By doing this you will be pouring more positive thoughts into your brain. Positive words such as:

I am confident.

I am gifted.

I am talented.

I am complete.

I am healthy.

I am dumping my trash.

I am dumping all of my trash.

I am dumping my trash right now.

I love my life.

I love my life.

I love my life.

You definitely can add more positive words to this list. When you say these words in the morning, you will feel a new spring in your step, and you will be ready to start your day like a racehorse out of the gate, moving toward a better future. If you don't have time to say all of these positive words, just say the last part: I love my life…I love my life…I love my life… Say it over and over and over again—even if you have a bad day. Fake it 'til you make it.

Now the question is, how can we keep this wonderful feeling for life? Studies show that we can add a new habit to our life, or get rid of some of our bad habits, in just twenty-one days. To be on the safe side, I say thirty days, but it must be done every day of those thirty days. If you skip one day, you have to start all over again. Once you do it for thirty days, most likely it will become a habit for you, and you will keep and enjoy it for life.

I recommend that for the next thirty days you say those positive words before you start your day. Discipline yourself to do it every day of those thirty days. Then it will become a habit, and you will enjoy it so much that you will want to do it for the rest of your life. By doing that you will be pouring positive thoughts into your brain on a daily basis, and the negative thoughts will overflow from the top.

4— At the same time, you have to stop negative and defeatist people from infecting your brain. Stay away from them.

It always gives me great joy to help people and to positively influence their lives, but negative people are a different situation. We have to be careful of them poisoning our lives. I have always tried to help them and create an environment for them to change themselves, but if they are not willing to make the changes, then I try to stay away from them. Negative people will take you down very fast. They will stop you from moving forward in life, and they will add dirty water to your bucket. Let me share a story with you that explains it really well.

Several years ago, I was traveling from South Korea to Las Vegas. If you had been sitting next to me on that plane, you would have experienced the most violent flight of your life.

I will never forget that dark night. We were flying

high in the sky. Suddenly, the plane started to shake violently. I had traveled overseas before, but I hadn't felt anything like that. It seemed like the plane was going to crash, and I could see the end of my life coming in a few short seconds.

Then the voice of the pilot came on the intercom and with a positive tone, he said, "Ladies and gentlemen, we are experiencing turbulence. Please be seated, and fasten your seat-belts. We are trying to take the plane to a higher altitude and soon we will be out of this bumpy ride. Relax, and enjoy the rest of your flight."

The positive voice of the pilot gave us hope that we would be all right, and after a few minutes, we did get out of that bumpy ride. His positive voice was like a light turned on in that dark and stormy night.

Have you ever had anyone in your life who created turbulence, caused bumpy rides, or attempted to add dirty water to your bucket? Unfortunately, most of us have, and some of us whole flocks of them.

How do we know if a person is positive? Well, it is very easy. I have a friend who is very positive.

Every time she enters the room you immediately feel it. The whole room becomes positive and vibrant. Everybody loves her.

How do we know if a person is negative? Well, that is easy, too. When a negative person enters the room, you immediately feel it. He or she sucks all of the positive energy out of everybody.

Positive voices give us hope and the energy to move forward and accomplish our goals, while negative voices tear us down.

My friend, fly high! Fly high like an eagle, and don't pay attention to those negative and defeatist people who are trying to bring you down. Have you ever seen an eagle come down and argue with the chickens on the ground? Never! You will never see that. The eagle may come down to eat the chickens, but definitely not to argue with them. Those negative and defeatist people who are trying to bring you down are like the chickens on the ground. Don't pay attention to them. If they insist on creating turbulence in your life, causing bumpy rides, and trying to add dirty water to your bucket, then do what that pilot from South Korea to Las Vegas did. Take yourself to a higher altitude, and fly high.

5— And most importantly, we have to forgive the people who have harmed us in the past, and stop hating them. People such as an ex-husband, ex-wife, ex-boyfriend, ex-girlfriend, parents, family members, or business partners. Sometimes we hate them so much that we cannot move forward in life, because we are wasting our precious positive energy on hating them. Unfortunately, that was my situation, too. I was carrying too much trash from the past, and I could not move forward in life.

Then, one day, I read a quotation by Nelson Mandela. He said, "Hating someone is like swallowing poison hoping it kills the other person." It was absolutely true in my case. That poison was killing me—not her. I realized I had to stop hating her, for my own good. It was hard, but I had to do it so I could move forward in life.

Forgiveness does not mean that you should trust that person or have a loving relationship again. Trust must be earned—but forgiveness means you set yourself free.

When I was a child, my father told me a story about a thief who entered the house of one of his friends. In the middle of the night, the owner of the house woke up and heard a noise in the living room. He came out of his room, and caught the thief. The thief started crying and begged him for forgiveness. The thief said, "I am a poor man, and I did it out of desperation." The owner of the house was a kind man, and he immediately forgave the thief. He gave him food to eat. He even let him sleep in the living room until morning. The owner went to his room to sleep, feeling great that he had done something good by helping someone who was so desperate.

When he woke up in the morning, he went directly to the kitchen to prepare breakfast for his special guest—the thief. Unfortunately, the guest was gone, and the living room was almost empty. The thief had taken all of the valuable items with him.

Don't confuse forgiveness for trust. You should forgive immediately and unconditionally. You should do it for your own good, but trust is something that the other person must earn. Forgiving the thief was honorable, but trusting him was questionable. You forgive the other person no matter how heinous the crime was, and you forgive him or her immediately. At the same time, you have to fight for your rights, fight against injustice, and stop people from abusing your kindness.

You have to forgive so you can be free.

You have to forgive so you can improve your overall physical and mental health.

You have to forgive so you can dump your trash, move forward, and discover a brighter future.

You have to forgive for your own good.

THE BUCKET THEORY

I call the above recommendations "The Bucket Theory"—keep pouring clean thoughts into your bucket, so that the negative thoughts can overflow from the top. Very soon, the brain that was full of bad memories, a painful past, and a negative mindset, will be replaced with a clean, positive, and fresh one. When you do that, you will love yourself and your new brain. Everything that flows from your mind will be inspirational and uplifting, like a breath of fresh air. By doing that you will be free from your past and you will be able to travel light to your exciting future.

SUMMARY

Now let me ask you this: Did you dump your trash? If you haven't done it by now, I recommend going back to the beginning of this chapter and reading it again. You don't want to move to the next chapter while still carrying the trash from your past. Remember the example of climbing the ladder in the construction business while carrying trash? You won't be able to move up the ladder in your life and career if you are carrying the heavy trash from your past. Also, remember my trip to Japan? You won't be able to go very far in life if you are carrying heavy trash from your past.

The past is gone. You cannot change it. Mistakes are made. You cannot unscramble eggs. The best you can do is to learn from your past, dump your trash, so you can move forward.

Whenever you are ready, flip to the next page, and let's continue our journey to your brighter future...a much brighter future.

Cardinal Rule #2:

Accept 100% Responsibility

Once, I built a house for a couple. It was an expensive one. In California, whenever a builder builds a house, he or she has to provide a one-year warranty. The builder has to go back and fix whatever needs to be fixed, such as plumbing, electrical, cracks in the floor tiles, and more.

About six months after they moved in, one morning the lady called me and with an angry voice she said, "Paul, the faucet in the kitchen is damaged. I need you to replace it immediately."

I said, "Wow! That is surprising." It was an expensive pull-out faucet, and this had never happened in the past. Luckily, I was working in that neighborhood. I told her, "I will be there shortly."

When I entered the house, the mood was different. The husband and wife were not talking to each other. I could sense that they had had a fight, and that someone had gotten angry and had pulled out the faucet and damaged it. Now she wanted me to install a new faucet for them for free!

I looked at the angry faces of the husband and wife, and I saw the stack of knives on the kitchen counter. I was scared. I told myself, "I better get out of here quickly. This place is not safe." I told the lady, "No problem, I will put a new faucet in for you." At that moment she could have asked for a brand new kitchen and I would have done it.

I thought the best way to handle that conflict was to Accept 100% Responsibility and install a new faucet. I also thought that it could have been my plumber's fault. Maybe he hadn't installed it properly.

I bought a new faucet, and I called my plumber to install it. It was done in the afternoon, and it looked nice. The lady came and checked the new faucet and thanked me for the fast service. In the afternoon, the mood in the house was better, and she was calmer and more relaxed. Before I left their house, I indirectly told her, "I know what happened, but I installed a new faucet for you anyway. Enjoy it." A few months later, she referred one of her friends to me to build a house for them.

When you Accept 100% Responsibility—even in a situation that is not your fault—then usually you will get rewarded in a different way, sometimes many times over. My recommendation is that instead of blaming your life's misery on others, why don't you Accept 100% Responsibility, even if it is not your fault? Plant the seed and reap the rewards later. By doing that, most of the time you will benefit from it tremendously—in a different way.

Unfortunately, we live in a society in which people are more concerned about their rights than about accepting full responsibility to fix the problem. Because of that, they blame other people. But winners, leaders, and champions accept more responsibility when they go through hardships, even if it is not their fault. As a result of that, they will be able to bounce back to a higher level of success. That is why we call them bosses, CEOs, business owners, and leaders, and that is why many of us work for them. They know that in order to get to the top, they have to Accept 100% Responsibility, even if it is not their fault.

WHY 100% ?

Now let me prove why responsibility has to be taken at a full 100%, not 75% or 90%. After graduating from college, first I worked as a civil engineer for a few years. A good example to prove that responsibility has to be taken 100% is that of a water dam. Yes, a water dam. Civil engineers spend months designing the structure of the dam, such as its thickness, height, foundation, and the reinforcements inside the structure. But when the dam is full of water and is under maximum pressure, a crack could open up and cause the collapse of the whole dam. Even if 99% of the structure of the dam is solid, a 1% flaw, or just one crack in the dam, could destroy the whole dam, and that has happened in the past.

The same thing is true in life. You could take 99% responsibility in your life, but that 1% flaw—or even less than 1%, just a crack at one corner of your life—could open up when your life is under pressure and cause the collapse of your life in a short time. That is why accepting 100% responsibility is essential.

If you are not taking care of your children, that is a crack in your dam. If you are taking long coffee breaks at workplace instead of focusing on your work, that is another crack. If you are not fulfilling your financial obligations, that is a crack, too. Very soon your dam will be full of cracks. Failure will be just a matter of time. When your life is under pressure from your work, family, or financial demands, those cracks may open up and cause the collapse of your life. That is why Accepting 100% Responsibility is the key to your success.

You may say, "Paul, I hate my job. I hate my boss. I don't even like my career field. I don't want to Accept 100% Responsibility at this job." To answer that, I have to say, "Today you are working for ABC Company. In five years you may be working for XYZ Company. But you will always be working for yourself. You have to Accept 100% Responsibility for your own good."

I don't think there is any other way to succeed in business and life except by accepting full responsibility. Can a mechanic run his business by taking 50% responsibility—fixing car brakes only 50% of the time? Can a pilot fly a plane by taking 75% responsibility—flying to the right cities only 75% of the time? Can a nurse give the correct injections to his or her patients only 90% of the time? Absolutely not! That is why there is only one way to succeed in life and in business, and that is by Accepting 100% Responsibility. Less than that is like waiting for a disaster to happen. It will only be a matter of time, like having a crack in the dam. It will eventually open up when your life is under pressure, and the damage could be catastrophic, beyond repair, and too late for recovery.

When you Accept 100% Responsibility, you will separate yourself from the average people on the street. You will belong to an elite group. You will be able to crush the obstacles on your path, reinvent yourself for success, and unleash **THE MILLIONAIRE WITHIN** you.

RUNNING A RED LIGHT

Accepting 100% Responsibility is essential in our daily life. It has to be an inseparable part of our life. It can't be on a hit-and-miss basis, just whenever we feel like it. That is like having cracks in the dam. We have to commit to it 24/7, at any time, and in any situation. Let me share a story with you.

About twenty years ago, one day I ran a red light. I still vividly remember it. It was a Monday morning, and I had several important errands to run for my business. My mind was everywhere. After my first appointment, as I was rushing to the next one, I ran the red light. Usually I consider myself to be a responsible driver, and running a red light is not acceptable to me, but it happened.

After running the red light, I nervously looked around to make sure that there were no police cars around me. To my surprise, there was one just to my left. He immediately turned on his flashing red lights and siren and guided me to park on the right side of the street. I angrily said to myself, "This is the last thing I wanted to happen. Now I have to pay a huge fine, it will go onto my driving record, and my insurance rates will rise. I wish I had been more responsible in driving."

I parked my car on the side of the street and the police officer parked right behind me. His red emergency lights were flashing the whole neighborhood, announcing the capture of a new criminal, and hopefully, teaching a good lesson to everyone.

I sat in my car waiting for the police officer. Those few minutes felt like an eternity. I had no place to run. I couldn't even deny or come up with any excuses. How could I? I ran a red light, and the officer was next to me.

As I was waiting for the police officer to get out of his car, a very unorthodox and totally outside the box idea came to my mind. I told myself, let's be creative. He is going to give me a ticket anyway. It is not going to get worse than that! Let's change the game plan and totally surprise him. It may work.

I took my driver's license, insurance, and registration cards out. I had them ready in my hand. I rolled down the window and anxiously waited for him to come to me.

He got out of his car, adjusted his belt, touched his gun, and then walked toward me like he was about to capture Al Capone. He wanted me to feel his presence. Believe me, I did, but he had no idea that he was about to meet a very strange driver.

When he came to me, before he opened his mouth to speak, I handed him the documents that I had in my hand. I immediately told him, "Officer, you don't have to say anything. I know what I did. I ran a red light and I Accept 100% Responsibility for it. To me, running a red light is a major traffic violation. I cannot believe what I did. I am ashamed of myself."

I then said, "Officer, there is only one way that I will learn a good lesson and make sure that this will not happen again, and that is for you to punish me harshly. Double the fine, or even triple it. That will teach me a goooood lesson."

The officer was speechless. He didn't know whether to issue me a traffic citation or take me to a mental hospital. A few minutes earlier he was acting like a mean sheriff in one of those western movies, and now he was like a kind friend trying to comfort me. With a calm and friendly voice he said, "Mr. Noor, this can happen to any of us. I am glad to see that you accept 100% responsibility for your traffic violation. Let me go check your driving record. I will be right back."

A few minutes later, he came back to me and said, "Mr. Noor, I checked your driving record. You are a very responsible driver. I will let you go this time, but be very careful. Running a red light, as you admitted, is a major traffic violation. Drive safely, and have a good day," and he left.

I immediately rolled up the window and screamed, "Yeeeees! Yeeeees! It worked! It worked!"

So, what is the moral of this story? Accept 100% Responsibility of everything you do in your life. If you fall short, then Accept 100% Responsibility to fix what you did wrong. Apologize to the other person, and do it immediately, before it gets out of control. When you do, you will be amazed to see how easily the other person will forgive you, and there will be a good chance that the outcome will turn in your favor—even…if you run a red light.

That incident taught me a great lesson about the importance of Accepting 100% Responsibility on a daily basis, 24/7, and in any situation. The kindness of that police officer and the lesson that I learned from the experience will remain with me forever.

ACCEPTING RESPONSIBILITY FOR MY STUTTERING

One of the symptoms of stuttering is that it has lots of ups and downs. One day I am fluent for no reason and another day I am down and struggling. Or I could be fluent for a week, and then struggle again. I believe it is the worst disability to have. It is like being given life for a day or a week, and then having that life taken away—and the process repeats over and over and over again. It is devastating!

It is different from other disabilities. A blind person knows that he or she is blind. After a while, that person will get used to it and learn how to live with it, but stuttering is brutal! Those ups and downs created so much tension in my life that it directly affected my family. I was dumping all of my anxieties on them instead of accepting responsibility for my stuttering. They had to live with that for years.

Back in 1989, an opportunity opened up in my life. I enrolled in an intensive stuttering therapy program called the "Successful Stuttering Management Program" at Eastern Washington University, in Cheney, Washington. It was a breakthrough in my life. It opened a new door to my future. I hoped to find the cure for my debilitating stuttering in that three-week workshop.

The head and founder of the program was Dr. Dorvan Breitenfeldt, a severe stutterer himself. Before I attended the program, he interviewed me over the phone. He clearly told me, "Paul, I want to make sure you know that there is no cure for your stuttering. We have been running this workshop for about thirty years, and we haven't seen even one stutterer who has been cured, but we will teach you the best techniques that you can use to manage your stuttering."

I was shocked when I heard that. The whole reason for me attending that workshop was to cure my stuttering. If Dr. Breitenfeldt—an expert in stuttering therapy—tells me that there is no cure, then there can be no way that I will reach my dream of becoming a professional speaker.

He then said something that changed the whole picture, gave me hope, and let me see the light at the end of the tunnel. He said, "Paul, over the past thirty years we have seen people who improved a lot. Those were the people who took full responsibility for their stuttering. They put stuttering on their own shoulders instead of blaming others. They put stuttering at the top of their list. Those people improved a lot."

That was the golden nugget I had been looking for, which led me to practically cure my incurable stuttering: Accepting 100% Responsibility for my stuttering instead of blaming it on others. It gave me a completely new vision.

But why should I accept responsibility for it? It had all started when I was about three years old. I had nothing to do with it. Why should I accept responsibility for something that wasn't even my fault? Because of that mindset, I hadn't been able to improve at all. All my life I had blamed my stuttering on my parents, the school system, neighbors, the government, and anybody and everybody except for the main person, ME. I was a victim of stuttering and it wasn't my fault. We all know that victims will never excel in life and will never live their dream lives. Why? Because victims never Accept 100% Responsibility to escape from their victim mentality. A victim never wins.

In that stuttering workshop I realized that the first crucial step in overcoming my stuttering was to Accept 100% Responsibility even if it wasn't my fault. When I did that, I began to gain fluency. Even though my stuttering never was cured, and I had to go back to the same workshop three more summers, my improvement was noticeable, and today I am living my dream life as a professional speaker.

Dr. Breitenfeldt set a great cornerstone in my life for my victory over stuttering, and in my life in general, and that was Accepting 100% Responsibility for something that wasn't even my fault. When I did that, miracles started to happen in my life. I mean miracles, not m-m-m-m-m-m-miracles.

SUMMARY

As you read in this chapter, I am a staunch believer in Accepting 100% Responsibility. This philosophy is the foundation for our success. Every time I conduct a seminar or give a keynote speech, I try to promote and emphasize it. It should be inseparable from your life. It should become part of your character—24/7—in your personal life, career, or business. Less than 100% means having cracks in the dam. Failures will be just a matter of time.

Now, let me ask you this: Are you willing to Accept 100% Responsibility? If not, I recommend that you go back to the beginning of this chapter and read it again. Otherwise, you won't be able to get very far. You will blame others for your failures. You will see yourself as a victim, and victims cannot win. People with a victim mentality can never live their dream lives, and they will remain victims for life. They are always waiting for a miracle to get them out of their miserable lives. Sadly, they don't know that Accepting 100% Responsibility is the miracle that they have been looking for.

If by now you have Dumped Your Trash, and have Accepted 100% Responsibility, then you are almost halfway to Reinventing Yourself for Success. Congratulations! Go and take a break, rest, relax, and come back when you are fresh to start the next and exciting chapter: Set Your Goals.

Cardinal Rule #3:

Set Your Goals

Successful people have purpose, direction, and goals for their lives. They know exactly where they are going. On the other hand, unsuccessful people have no goals for their lives. Most of them have no idea where they will be in five years, or even one year. Their main concern is how to pay bills—forget about having goals. If you ask them if they have any goals for their lives, they will tell you, "I am too busy making ends meet. I don't have time for setting goals."

Unfortunately, they don't know that one of the reasons that they are not successful is that they don't have any goals for their lives. Instead of having their own goals, they are part of successful people's goals.

Rich and successful people set their goals, and poor and unsuccessful people work for them and get paid wages to make a living. To be successful in your life, you must have your own goals instead of working for someone else's goal. In this chapter, you will learn in detail how to Set Your Goals.

A LIFE WITHOUT GOALS CAN BE DISASTROUS

I remember it like it was just yesterday. Let me take you back to November 15, 1985. I was standing in front of a small, empty office in Visalia, California. For the first time, I turned the key in the door lock and walked into that empty room. I immediately hung a sign that I had with me on the window. It read: Paul Noor, Civil Engineer—Owner. At that time I had a very clear goal on the horizon and I was moving toward it like an arrow. I was motivated. I was unstoppable. Very soon, everybody around me was calling me "The Motivator."

Before I started my business, I wrote my goals on a piece of paper. In the first few years, I worked myself to the bone. Soon I reached all of my goals. Finally, I was able to relax. I didn't have to work as hard. I was spending more time with friends, waking up later in the morning, and watching a few more hours of television every night. I was really enjoying my life—no more goals, no direction, and absolutely no purpose in my life.

Gradually, I noticed some changes in myself. I wasn't as motivated as before. I lost the passion in my life. I got severely depressed, and the people around me were no longer calling me "The Motivator."

I was feeling so bad that I had to see a psychiatrist. He immediately put me on medication. That made me even worse. I was feeling like something terrible was going on with me. I told myself, "When I entered that empty office for the first time and hung my sign on the window, I felt like I was standing on the mountain top of my life.

Now, I am feeling like I am at the bottom of a black hole—in complete darkness."

Then, one day, when I was alone at home, I decided to end the misery that I was going through. I went to the bathroom and I poured all my pills into the palm of my hand. I contemplated my situation for a few minutes, and I kept coming back to the same conclusion: I had to end it all. I took a long, deep breath so I could muster every ounce of energy to complete the mission. Finally…

At the last moment, I dumped all of the pills into the toilet and immediately flushed them before I could change my mind. Deep down, I knew that my cure was not in taking those pills or visiting the psychiatrist. My problem was that I had no more goals in life, no direction, and no purpose. I had nothing to look forward to.

I ran to my office, and I immediately started writing a new goal to take me to the next level. I called my team and planned to start a construction project so that I could get myself moving again. For the next few months I dedicated my life to my new goal. Shortly after that, I got my joy back. I became motivated. I became unstoppable. Very soon, the people around me were calling me "The Motivator" again. I had gotten my title back because I had set a new goal for my life.

It doesn't matter if we are twenty, fifty, or eighty years old. We all need goals and direction so we can move forward in life. History is full of successful people who retired early and soon became severely depressed because they no longer had a goal in their lives. To escape their misery, they had to set another goal for themselves and go back to work again. How long can you relax on the beach? How many months can you vacation? How long can you sit on the couch and watch television? Healthy people won't be able to take it for very long. They will be lonely. They will lose their friends, because everyone else is working.

I have heard that complete retirement is like an early trip to the grave. I believe that is true. Part of the reason could be that they have no reason to get out of bed in the morning. They have no goals, no direction, and no purpose in life.

A good example is Michelangelo. He died at the age of eighty-nine, and that was about five hundred years ago, when the average life expectancy was about forty years. Michelangelo had goals in his life. He would climb to the top of the scaffolding, while lying on his back, he would paint the ceiling of the Sistine Chapel. Michelangelo had something to look forward to every day. He definitely had clear goals for his life.

DRIVING IN THE FOG

Someone said that not having goals and direction in life is like driving in the fog. I agree with that 100% because I have experienced it.

When I was in the construction business in central California, the distance from my house to the construction sites was about fifty-five miles. Sometimes I had to leave home at around five in the morning so that I could be in my office before my construction crew showed up.

Sometimes in November, December, and January, there was heavy fog in the morning. It was so thick that I could drive only about ten to twenty miles an hour on the freeway. I couldn't see very far. It was quite foggy and dangerous. One time, a pile-up of over a hundred cars occurred and more than hundred people were injured and a few died. The reason for the massive accident was that people couldn't see where they were going. Their targets were not clear.

Usually the fog would clear up in the afternoon. It was beautiful. I could see everywhere, and I was driving seventy-five miles an hour. I was driving like an arrow. I knew where I was going. I could see the target. The difference was huge.

The same thing is true in life. If you don't have a clear idea of where you are heading in life, it will be like driving in the thick fog in central California. You will be moving very slowly. You could take the wrong exit and head in a totally different direction. Driving in the heavy fog in central California will not get you very far, and living life without goals will not get you very far in your life, either.

GROWING MY ANNUAL INCOME FROM ZERO TO $500,000

In the year 2000, after several family and business setbacks, I decided to restart my construction business. I was way down, and in debt. So I decided to get back on my feet the same way I started my business back in 1985—with a goal.

This time my goal was very clear: to grow my annual income "from Zero to $500,000" within five years. People laughed at me. They probably thought I was nuts. With all my debt, how could I reach a yearly income of $500,000, especially as my previous income had averaged only $75,000? Almost everybody was laughing—except me. I knew the power of having a goal. I loved my family, and I was willing to do anything to provide a comfortable life for them.

I drew my goal on a chart and I pasted it on the wall. I looked at my goal every day before going to work and before going to bed at night. I even drew it on a small piece of paper and I kept it in my wallet. During the day, any time that I got depressed, I looked at my goal. It gave me the energy to move forward. I looked at it over and over and over again until I believed in it. Until my goal and I merged together. Until my goal became part of me, and I took action toward it on a daily basis.

My first year's goal, which was marked on the chart, was to have $50,000 income, and I made only $29,000.

In my second year, I almost reached my target income for that year: $100,000.

In my third year, I broke through the chart, and in my fifth year I reached my goal and I made over $500,000.

If it wasn't for the clear goal and chart that I had drawn for my construction business, I would have never been able to reach my goal. My goal was clear, specific, exciting, and it had a deadline. My one goal was to reach the income that I had written on the chart—and I did it. Luckily, the construction industry between 2000 and 2005 was very lucrative and created great opportunities for me to reach my goal. It was a blessing.

HOW TO SET YOUR GOALS?

After many years in the business, I came up with this simple technique for setting goals:

"The secret of setting your goals is in the SEAT that you are sitting on."

That statement is mine, and you can quote me on that. Yes, if you want to Set Your Goals, I recommend that you sit down, take out a piece of paper and a pen, and remember, "The secret in setting your goals is in the SEAT that you are sitting on." What I will be talking about here is not new. All experts in goal setting have been teaching and using these steps for years. I have just put them in a different format. Let me explain:

SPECIFIC

The letter "S" in the word SEAT stands for Specific.

All experts in setting and achieving goals believe that goals have to be specific. You should know exactly what you want.

When you ask some people about their goals, they may say, "I want to lose weight" or "I want to be a good salesperson." I am afraid to say that those are not goals. They are just dreams and wishes. You have to say:

"This month I want to lose ten pounds"—very specific.

"This year I want to be ranked among the top five salespeople in our company."

If the goal is not specific and clear, you won't be able to reach it. It will be like driving in the foggy weather in central California where I was living. That is why your goal has to be specific.

EXCITING

The letter "E" in the word SEAT stands for Exciting.

Goals must be exciting. If a goal is not exciting, it will not give you any energy to do anything about it. One of the reasons that most people don't accomplish their goals is because their goals are not exciting. Their goals are very easy. There is nothing special about them.

Your goal must give you so much excitement that you cannot wait to get out of bed in the morning. Your goal should give you so much excitement that every day you want to do something to get one step closer to it.

If your goal is to read one book per year, that is not exciting. Most likely, you will wait until December to read it. If you set a goal to read one book per month, that will be exciting.

If your goal is to lose ten pounds in one year, that is not exciting. It does not stretch you. It is not challenging. But if you set a goal of losing ten pounds in one month, then that will be exciting.

If the goal is too easy—no excitement—you won't grow. The goal must be exciting.

ACHIEVABLE

The letter "A" in the word SEAT stands for Achievable.

If your goal is to go back to school to get your master's degree in one semester, that is not achievable. But getting your master's degree in two years is achievable.

If your goal is to start a business and to become a millionaire in one year, that is not achievable—at least not in most cases. But if your goal is to start a business and to retire comfortably in ten years, then that is achievable.

If your goal is to lose fifty pounds in one month, that is not achievable. But losing fifty pounds with the help of professionals, with proper diet and exercise, over a period of several months is achievable.

TIMEFRAME

The letter "T" in the word SEAT stands for Timeframe.

Having a deadline is important. A deadline will give you purpose to take action and to reach your goals. If there is no timeframe for completing your goals, then you will never finish them, because you know that you have plenty of time. Why finish them now? You can finish them next week, or next month, or even next year. Deadlines create excitement and urgency. They give you purpose to move forward and to reach your goals on time.

For example, imagine that we could live forever. It would be boring. Our life is exciting because we know there is a time limit attached to it. We know we will live to be eighty or a hundred years old. If we could live forever, we would never get anything done. We would procrastinate the whole time. You could say, "Mom, why should I go to kindergarten now? I am only a hundred years old! My neighbor Johnny went to kindergarten when he was two hundred years old! I have plenty of time. Why rush? I will live forever!"

Life without a time limit attached to it would be horrible! Nothing would get done! The reason that people are accomplishing things in life, going to college, starting businesses, and enjoying their lives is that there is a deadline in life. Deadlines give us excitement and urgency to achieve our goals. A goal without a timeframe is just like a dream.

Let me restate these four characteristics of successful goal setting. As I mentioned earlier, "The secret of setting your goals is in the SEAT that you are sitting on."

The letter "S" means that your goal must be Specific.

The letter "E" means that your goal must be Exciting.

The letter "A" means that your goal must be Achievable.

The letter "T" means that your goal must have a Timeframe for completion.

Now let's see if my goal of growing my yearly income "from Zero to $500,000" had these qualities.

"S"— My goal was to increase my income to a very Specific amount: $500,000 per year.

"E"— My goal definitely was Exciting. Do you know anyone who doesn't get excited by the idea of his or her income going "from Zero to $500,000"?

"A"— Was the goal Achievable? If you had asked other people, the answer would have been no. The goal was not achievable, but since I knew the power of setting goals, and especially since I had experienced it when I started my business, I knew that it would be achievable. Yes, to other people it was not. It was just a fantasy, but to me it was achievable. In fact, I have to say that if everybody feels that your goal is achievable, it means that your goal is probably too small. It is too easy to achieve. So the fact that people didn't see it as being achievable indicated that it was a big goal for me, and that is good because I had to stretch myself to reach it. It means that my goal was exciting.

"T"— Did my goal have a Timeframe? Absolutely! It was a five-year plan. I was supposed to have an income of $500,000 per year in just five years. I knew exactly by when I needed to achieve it, and I did.

YOU MUST
WRITE DOWN YOUR GOALS

Unfortunately, it is very hard to focus on our goals because there are so many distractions around us. As I mentioned earlier, research shows that every day, over fifty thousand thoughts go through our minds. It means that we have lots of distractions on a daily basis. One of the best ways to stay focused on your goals is to write them down on a piece of paper and read them daily.

I recommend that you read them three times per day: first thing in the morning, noontime, and in the evening before going to sleep. When you lose focus and get distracted, off track, or depressed, read your goals again. Very quickly, this will set you in the right direction. Writing down your goals and reading them daily is a great way to stay focused and to keep yourself on the right track.

TAKE DAILY ACTION TOWARD YOUR GOAL

As soon as you set your goal, take action toward it on a daily basis. It doesn't have to be a big action. Just a small action will give you the momentum and motivation to move forward toward your goal. This way, you will feel good about yourself because you have accomplished something. Small daily actions will lead to bigger actions, and they will keep reminding you of your final goal.

For example, if your goal is to lose weight, then when you go to a fast food restaurant, don't supersize the French fries and soft drink. Or, if your goal is to pay off your credit cards in six months, or your house in six years, then put an empty jar on the shelf, and every night empty your pockets, and place your change into it. This will remind you of your final goal and will give you the motivation to accomplish your goal in a shorter time.

FOCUS ON YOUR GOAL LIKE A LASER BEAM

After setting a clear goal, you must then focus on it like a laser beam. Let me explain. The sun releases tons of energy and yet we can walk outside under the sun and it doesn't burn us. On the other hand, a laser beam uses a very small amount of energy and can destroy a rock. Why? Because the energy of the laser beam is focused, while the energy of the sun is not. If you want to reach your goal, you have to gather all of your energy and focus it on your goal like a laser beam. This way you will vaporize all obstacles in front of you as you move forward.

If you have too many goals and projects going on at the same time, you won't get very far. That is what I was doing at the beginning. I wanted to overcome my stuttering, be a professional speaker, write a book, stay in the construction business, learn sales techniques, train and uplift other people, build orphanages in poor counties, and a few other things. I was like a hundred-watt light bulb shining light in all directions. I was not focused on any one thing. I was like a jack-of-all-trades and a master of none. I wasn't getting anywhere in life.

On the other hand, a laser beam uses less energy yet is so powerful that it vaporizes a rock. It performs magic, especially in the scientific and medical fields. It saves lives, but a hundred-watt bulb is very common and ordinary. There is nothing special about it. You can go to the local store and buy a bunch of them. No one will say to you, "Wow! I love your hundred-watt bulb. Where did you buy it?" They are very cheap, and there is nothing exciting about them. In order for you to reinvent yourself for success and unleash **THE MILLIONAIRE WITHIN** you, you must focus on your goal like a laser beam, and definitely not like a hundred-watt bulb.

PUT YOUR GOAL AT THE
TOP OF YOUR LIFE

As I mentioned earlier, in 1989, I started receiving my intensive stuttering therapy. There is no cure for stuttering, at least for my level of stuttering. But I can say that my control over my stuttering was greater than that of other students in the stuttering workshop that I attended. I believe it was mainly because I put control of my stuttering at the top of my list. It was the most important thing in my life— more important than my wife, sons, parents, family, and friends. Everything else was secondary. I directed most of my energy toward overcoming my stuttering. I was attacking it like a laser beam.

Everybody thought that I was very selfish. How could I put my wife, children, and family in second place? I did it because I knew that if I didn't direct most of my energy toward my stuttering, I would never be able to manage it. It is an incurable speech disorder. There was only one way I could achieve a meaningful improvement, and that was to attack it like a laser beam and crush it. I knew that if I did not control my stuttering, it would control me. I knew that if I could manage my stuttering, I would

71

be a better husband, a more caring father, and a better friend. That is why I basically cut myself off from everything that was not related to my stuttering—so that I could use most of my energy like a laser beam to break it into pieces.

At the time of writing this book, my stuttering is not cured, and most likely it never will be. I have to do daily exercises to manage it, but it is still at the top of my list. Everything else is secondary. Because of that, I am able to manage it better than other stutterers. Today I present business seminars and speaking to groups of people. This is proof that when you put your goal at the top of your list, and focus on it like a laser beam, you can crush the most vicious obstacles in your path—even incurable stuttering.

DON'T CONFUSE YOUR BRAIN

One of the reasons that most people are not successful and not living their dream life is because they are not clear and focused on their goals, and they are giving mixed messages to their brains.

One day they get excited and want to be at the top, and the next day they say, "Ahhh…it is hard work to be at the top."

One day they see a beautiful car and get excited about working hard to buy it. The next day they say, "Ahhh…there is nothing wrong with my old pickup. Still runs."

One day they realize that it is important to have enough money for retirement. The next day they say, "Ahhh…if I get rich, other people will ask me to help them."

Because they are giving these mixed messages to their brains, they are not able to reach the top. Successful people, on the other hand, are very focused on the fact that they want to be at the top. They want to be at the top every day of the year. They want to be at the top all the time, and because of that, they are at the top.

FROM STUTTERING TO PROFESSIONAL SPEAKING

After the collapse of my marriage and the loss of my construction business, I set a new goal in my life. My new goal was this: To overcome my debilitating stuttering and go "From Stuttering to Professional Speaking," and to write a book about my journey that would help others. My target date was to achieve it within five years.

My new goal in life was very unorthodox and outside of the box. What are the chances of a stutterer becoming a keynote speaker and corporate trainer? I had tried many times in the past, and I had failed many times. This time, my situation was even worse than before. I was over fifty, I was practically broke, I had lost my construction business, and the housing market in central California had collapsed. I was homeless, living at motels and on friends' couches. There was no room for error. Whatever I was doing had to be on target. I could not drive in the fog.

No one believed in me except for myself. The people who had doubts about my new journey didn't know the power of having goals.

Several years earlier I had set a goal of increasing my yearly income "From Zero to $500,000" within five years. I had set that goal and I had achieved it. With the same beliefs, I now set a goal for my new dream life. I knew that the only way to get back on my feet would be to set a goal immediately, and I did.

I used the same formula that I discussed earlier: "The secret of setting your goals is in the SEAT that you are sitting on."

"S" for Specific

"E" for Exciting

"A" for Achievable

"T" for Timeframe

Now, let's see if my goal had all of these components:

"S"— I set a very Specific goal—to become a professional speaker.

"E"— My goal was outside of the box, and it definitely was Exciting.

"A"— Was my goal Achievable? To most people it was not, but to me it was achievable. I had achieved goals before, and I knew the power of setting goals.

"T"— Did my goal have a Timeframe? Absolutely! I was supposed to achieve it within five years. As I write this book, four years have passed, and I am already speaking professionally. If I had not had any Timeframe for my goal, I wouldn't have been able to accomplish it.

And of course, I wrote down my goal, and I read it daily. Every time I was depressed or distracted from my goal, I read it again, and again, and again. That would put me back on the right track. It was in my wallet, it was pinned to the wall next to my bed, and it was taped to the steering wheel of my car so that I could see it all the time. I was constantly reminding myself of my new goal in life. I was focusing on my goal like a laser beam, and every day I was taking a small action toward achieving it. Finally, I reached my goal.

SEVEN DAYS WITH JACK CANFIELD

A few years ago, I attended a seven-day workshop given by Mr. Jack Canfield, the famous coauthor of *Chicken Soup for the Soul*. That workshop was one of the best experiences of my life. During the workshop, we had to set a goal that we wanted to achieve in five years. Throughout the program, in addition to giving us a wonderful talk, Jack Canfield walked us through our dream goals: how to set them, and how to achieve them. The most interesting part was on the last night. Our instructions were to meet in the ballroom, dressed for success in our intended profession. We were to act as if we had already reached our dream goal. On that night, we had to fast-forward the clock by five years.

My goal was to be an author and keynote speaker within five years. In the Jack Canfield workshop, I set a clear goal for my life, and on the last night, acting and living my dream life sealed the deal. That night, I made a promise to Jack Canfield and four hundred students in the workshop that I would be living my dream life in five years. I had a clear mission in life, and I had five years to complete it.

It was fascinating to see everybody dressed appropriately for his or her profession. One person wanted to be a famous chef, and he dressed in a chef's outfit. Another wanted to be a model, and she dressed in fashionable clothing. One person wanted to be a successful financial advisor, so he walked around talking to everyone about the different opportunities that he could offer. And I walked through the crowd introducing myself as an author and keynote speaker. I talked about and marketed my new book—the book that I was going to publish in five years. That night was absolutely one of the best experiences of my life—living my dream life, five years in advance.

Less than four years later, I am writing this book. I am one year ahead of my target date, and I am already living my dream life, as I promised everyone in that workshop.

SUMMARY

Now, let me ask you this, did you Set Your Goals? Did you use the guidelines that I discussed in this chapter? If you did't, I recommend that you go back to the beginning of this chapter and read it again, until you make the commitment to it, and only then move to the next chapter. Without having a clear goal and direction, life will be like driving in the fog in central California. You won't go very far, and you may take the wrong exit.

I am sure that by now, you agree with me that having clear goals is a MUST. Write down your goal, and read it three times per day. Every day, take a small action toward achieving it. Put your goal at the top of your to-do list. Focus on your goal like a laser beam, so that you can vaporize the obstacles in your path, and before you sleep at night, close your eyes and visualize the life that you want to live.

When you reach this level of dedication and commitment, half of your battle is over. Congratulations! Look at the horizon: by now you should be able to see the beautiful life that you have been longing for. At this stage, no one can stop you from reaching it.

When you are ready and fresh, flip to the next chapter, which is about Building Your Deep Foundation. I will be anxiously waiting for you.

Cardinal Rule #4:

Build Your Deep Foundation

I have always been fascinated with people who came from rough beginnings, lifted themselves up, and now stand taller than the crowd, and with people who fell down from the top, but shortly after, got themselves back on their feet, and were able to stand even taller than before. I have always been eager to know what is the secret of standing tall, and how tall we can stand in life. Amazingly, I found the answer to this question in a very strange way. I found it in my engineering and construction business. I found out that the secret to standing tall in life is the same as in building a tall and beautiful high-rise. Yes…the same. Let me explain.

In my construction business, when I was building a single story home, the crew would dig continuous footing about one foot deep around the perimeter of the house. If the house was two stories, then the footing would be about two feet deep. If the building was four or five stories, then the footing would be even deeper. As you can see, the taller the building, the deeper the foundation.

The same thing is true when it comes to how tall we want to stand in life. The taller we want to stand in life, the deeper we have to build our foundation of personal development. If you want to be an average person, then what you have learned in high school and college will be enough. But if you want to stand taller than the crowd, to shine above the best of the best, then you have to work on your deep foundation of personal development.

Once I saw a construction crew digging extremely deep for the foundation of a high-rise building. It was a massive foundation project, with a huge investment. From my engineering background I knew that this deep foundation was needed so that they could build that tall and beautiful high-rise on top of it. As you can see: the taller the building, the deeper the foundation. The taller you want to stand in life, the deeper you have to build your foundation of personal development. It means that you have to commit yourself to lifelong learning.

A good example is Frank Lloyd Wright, the famous American architect. Toward the end of his career, someone asked him, "Mr. Wright, among all those beautiful buildings that you designed around the world, which one is your best project?"

Mr. Wright answered, "My next project. My next project will be my best project." Because Mr. Wright believed that no matter how good we are in our field, we have to learn all the time; we have to raise our bar of excellence all the time. Because Mr. Wright believed that no matter how good we are in our field, our best project always has to be our next project. Our best product always has to be our next product, and our best life always has to be in front of us—not behind us.

Unfortunately, some people may say, "Paul, we are done with our education. It is time to make money and enjoy life," and they proudly hang their diplomas on the wall. Do you know how many of those college degrees that people hang on their walls are outdated? Probably most of them. I have a master's degree from thirty years ago. If I relied on that, I would be starving.

We live in a very competitive world. High-rises are getting taller all the time, people are standing taller all the time, and the bar of excellence keeps rising higher all the time. Back in 1889, the construction of the beautiful Eiffel Tower was completed. For many years it was the tallest building in the world, and they had to dig deep for its foundation. Then the Empire State Building held the world record for many years. Now, at the time of writing this book, the tallest building in the world is in Dubai. They had to dig very deep for its foundation. As you can see, the taller the building, the deeper the foundation. The taller you want to stand in life, the deeper you have to build your foundation of personal development.

I have to mention that there is a big difference between building a foundation in the construction business and building the foundation for your personal development. When the construction crew builds the foundation for a high-rise, it will never change. They will not modify or reinforce it after it has been completed—except in very special cases. But in life, we have to constantly reinforce the foundation of our personal development while we are reaching our goals, and we have to improve and reinforce it for the rest of our lives. As I said, learning must be a lifelong commitment, because everything else around us is changing.

My recommendation is to read at least one nonfiction book per month. Go to seminars, workshops, and classes regularly. Commit yourself to lifelong learning, and keep working on your deep foundation of personal development. When you do that, very soon you will stand taller than the crowd, shine above the best of the best, and you will be able to reach your goal and live your dream life.

Now, the question is: How tall do you want to stand in life? It's all up to you.

YOU COULD BE OFF BY
ONLY HALF AN INCH

Several years ago I hired a tennis coach to teach me how to serve better. Although I had been playing tennis in the past, serving was one of my weaknesses. Sometimes I was off by about five feet.

During my first lesson, my coach asked me to serve a few times, and I did. I don't have to tell you what happened. I couldn't hit the target. I told him, "You see coach, I am way off—sometimes by five feet."

He smiled at me and said, "Paul, you are not off by five feet. You are off by Only Half an Inch."

I said, "Coach, thank you very much for the kind words, but I really want to learn how to serve better. I am ready to start."

He said, "Paul, you are not listening to me. If you don't listen, you won't learn. I told you, you are not off by five feet. You are off by Only Half an Inch."

I said, "Coach, what do you mean I am off by Only Half an Inch? Didn't you see that?"

He said, "Paul, listen. Please listen. If you make

half an inch of improvement in the way that you are holding the racket, half an inch of improvement in the way that you are hitting the ball, and a few minor improvements in the rotation of your body, those few minor adjustments will give you huge outcomes at the other end, and you will be able to move the ball by five feet or more in either direction and hit the target."

Wooooow! What a great life lesson! A few minor improvements in me will give me huge outcomes at the other end. If this simple principle works in tennis, it can work in our personal life, career, and business, too. And that is one of the most valuable lessons that I have learned in my life.

To me, it is even more important for us to work on these minor improvements than it is for professional tennis players. Because in tennis, the court is fixed. The length of the court is fixed. The width of the court is fixed. The height of the net is fixed. Even with all of these elements being fixed, professional tennis players constantly work on their minor improvements.

In life, career, or business, the court that we are

playing on is changing all the time. Because the world is changing all the time. The economy is changing all the time. The knowledge of the world is changing all the time. One day we are playing on a concrete court, the next day on a clay court, and another day we could be playing on a very rough and uneven court.

This is why we have to constantly educate ourself and work on these minor improvements so that we will be ready to hit the target no matter how rough or uneven the court of life gets.

So, if your life, your career, or your business is not going the way that you desire, or if you haven't reached your goals yet, remember, you could be off by Only Half an Inch.

GET ADVICE ONLY FROM EXPERTS

I have a piece of advice for you: Get advice only from experts.

If you need advice in order to reach your goals, don't try to get help from your Uncle Joe, your neighbor, or just anyone you meet. They may be good in their own field but not in yours. Some people cannot even run their own lives, but they sure are good at giving advice to others. Always get experts' opinions.

In my business, I try to meet many accomplished people in my field, and I stay in touch with them. When I need advice or assistance, I call them, meet them, pay them, or take them to lunch or dinner, and I receive their expert opinions.

My point is, to reinvent yourself for success, always get advice from experts. If you consult with everyone you meet, you may head in the wrong direction, lose your focus, and get very confused. I heard a great old story that explains it really well.

The story is about an old man and his grandson who decided to take a trip from their village into town. They took their donkey and started the journey. The grandfather let his grandson ride the donkey, and he walked alongside them.

Someone walked by and said, "That's ridiculous! The poor old man is walking and the boy is riding the donkey. What has happened to our world? Nobody respects the elderly anymore."

The old man heard that, and he took the boy off the donkey. He then rode the animal, and the young boy walked alongside.

Shortly afterward, another person came by and said, "Look at that selfish old man riding the donkey with the young boy walking on the side. What a shame! How can he do such a thing? He has no compassion for that young boy."

The old man got embarrassed when he heard that. He picked up the boy and put him on the back of the donkey. Now both of them were riding the animal. He thought, "Now, nobody will get upset," and they continued their journey.

After a few minutes, another person came along. This time, the comments were even worse: "What a cruelty! That poor donkey has to carry the old man and the boy."

By the time they got to town, the grandfather and the grandson were carrying the donkey.

What is the point of this story? Get advice only from experts; otherwise, at the end of your journey to reach your goals, you may be carrying the donkey, too.

LEARN PUBLIC SPEAKING

As part of educating yourself and deepening your foundation, I recommend learning the art of public speaking. If you have a good idea but you cannot express yourself, then that good idea doesn't mean much. When you stand up in front of people and speak eloquently, people will respect you. They will listen to you. They will love to do business with you and follow you as a leader, and that is priceless! If I could go "From Stuttering to Professional Speaking," then you can, too.

The best way to learn the art of public speaking is to join a Toastmasters Club. Go to www.toastmasters.org and find the club nearest you. I have been a member for several years, and it has worked magic in my life and my career. Clubs typically meet once a week or once every two weeks, and they offer a supportive, non-judgmental environment for practicing speeches and other types of communication.

Toastmasters International is a nonprofit organization that started in the United States in 1924 and is now all over the world. Visit a few clubs and see which one you like the most. For example, at one time I was a member of four different Toastmasters clubs. I wanted to practice my speeches in front of four different audiences so that I could get four different sets of feedback.

One was a very advanced club. Most of the members were professional attorneys, executives, college professors, real estate agents, and other accomplished speakers. Some had been members of that club for more than thirty years. It really was an advanced club. It stretched me really far. If you are not an advanced speaker, joining a club like that can be intimidating.

Another club was for beginners. It was a very comfortable and relaxing environment. The members of that club were friendly and they looked for opportunities to help the newcomers. The best way to choose a club is to visit a few of them and join the club that is right for you.

I strongly believe that if you want to reinvent yourself for success, if you want to advance in life, or if you want to be a leader in your community, you have to be a good communicator. Some of you may say, "Paul, public speaking is a skill that people are born with. It is not a learnable skill." In response, I have to say that although some leaders such as John F. Kennedy, Martin Luther King Jr., and Ronald Reagan probably were born with public speaking talents, the good news for the rest of us is that public speaking is a learnable skill. Again, if I could do it, then you can, too.

GIVE FREE SPEECHES TO REACH YOUR GOALS

A great way to reinvent yourself for success and reach your goals is to give free speeches. Many organizations such as Rotary Clubs, Lions Clubs, and other nonprofit organizations are always looking for speakers. They meet regularly, and they need speakers all the time. Members of those clubs are usually leaders in their community. Go there, give free speeches, sell your ideas, grow your business, and reach your goals. I have spoken at their clubs many times. Their members are the nicest people on the planet. You definitely should meet them.

Let me emphasize that your mission is to give a free speech and to network. Do not try to sell your products or services. For example, if you own a car dealership, talk about how to negotiate the purchase of a new car, the differences between leasing a car and buying one, or talk about some of the upcoming technologies in the car industry.

Don't talk about the special sale that you will have over the weekend by saying, "Hey everybody, this weekend you can buy a brand new Toyota with no money down, and we only have five left. First come, first served." No, no, no... When you give a sales pitch, you turn off everybody. You will ruin your own reputation. Give free speeches, help the community, build up your network, grow your business, and reach your goals. If members see that you are honestly trying to help them, they will come to help your business—maybe by buying one of those last five Toyotas left on the planet that you claim to have on your car lot.

When I started my speaking business, I gave numerous free speeches at Rotary and Lions Clubs to improve my speaking skills. One night after my speech, a lady in the audience came to me and said, "Paul, I really loved your presentation. I would like to invite you to be the keynote speaker at our upcoming convention." That was my first keynote speech, and she paid me fairly.

Another time, I gave a speech about construction and development, which is my expertise. After the meeting, a man approached me and talked to me about a piece of property that he had. He was thinking of building on it. I had given a free speech to help the community, and I ended up with a construction lead. As you can see, free speeches are not really free—they are an investment for your future.

Learn the art of public speaking and watch yourself blossom. Being able to speak eloquently in front of other people is priceless. You will be light-years ahead of your competition, and you will be able to reach your goals much faster.

HOW TO COME UP WITH GREAT IDEAS

All of my life, I have worked very hard to make a living, yet some people come up with just one good idea that makes them successful in life. I wish I could come up with a great idea! Does this sound familiar to you?

I like to teach a wonderful technique that will make your dream come true. You will learn that you have always been a genius with great ideas— you just never learned to uncover them.

I have always believed that hard work is essential to our success, but in reality, the people who make a fortune are those with great ideas. We live in a very competitive world. If you want to stay ahead of the pack, you must have a better idea than your competitors. Now the question is, how do you come up with good ideas?

One evening I came home from work and I was very tired. I told my brain, "Listen, I am tired of working hard and not getting anywhere in life. You have to come up with some good ideas."

My brain said, "Hey, wait a minute. I have been hibernating for most of my life. I have never learned to give you good ideas."

I said, "That is why I am not getting anywhere in life, because you have been lazy. Listen, the key to success is for you to work hard, not me. That's it! Get back to work! I need one idea every day, and I am damn serious!"

I immediately bought a small tape recorder so I could capture those ideas, because ideas can come to us at any time. If we don't capture them, a minute later they may be gone. This tape recorder was always with me.

I waited…and waited…and waited. Nothing happened. Not even one idea. I went back to my brain and said, "Hey you, where are those ideas?"

My brain said, "Paul, how can I come up with good ideas? All my life, you made me watch a few hours of television every night while you were eating popcorn. You made me associate with your lazy friends who were complaining all the time. You never even bought a good book for me to read. How can I give you good ideas? You never even exposed me to good ideas."

Wow! That hit me like a ton of bricks, "You never even exposed me to good ideas." I then remembered the story of a man who told his wife he was going fishing at the lake near their house. A few hours later, he proudly came back with a salmon in his hand. His wife took it to the kitchen to cook it for dinner. While she was preparing the salmon, she found the price tag attached to it.

What is the point of this story? If you want to catch salmon, you have to go where the salmon are. You don't go to the lake next to your home—otherwise you will have to buy one from your local grocery store and pretend that you caught it.

If you want to come up with good ideas, you have to go to where the good ideas are. You have to expose yourself to good ideas—by reading books, going to workshops and seminars, joining different clubs and organizations, and by associating yourself with smart people who have good ideas. That is exactly what I did. Shortly after, ideas started coming. They were not great ideas, but at least they were coming.

Let me share with you some of the ideas I wrote down at the beginning:

— Today, I made the commitment to do at least a thirty-minute power walk in the morning.

— No matter how busy I am, I should take one day off per week to rejuvenate myself.

— My neighbor is a very negative person. I should encourage him to accept that job out of state and get him out of this area.

— I came up with this quotation: The taller the building, the deeper the foundation. The taller you want to stand in life, the deeper you have to build your foundation of personal development.

— I think more clearly early in the morning. Beginning tomorrow, I will wake up at five in the morning and devote the first hour of my day to my reading and writing.

As you can see, these are not great ideas. Gradually, I was getting better ideas, mainly about my goals and future. Then one day, my brain came up with a great idea for a huge shopping center project. It could be a gold mine, so, of course, I am not going to share it with you in this book. I am just waiting for the right investor. If you come up with one idea every day, there is a chance that, in the course of one year, some of those ideas could be valuable, and one of those could be the golden nugget that you have been looking for.

Let me emphasize that in order for your brain to blossom with good ideas, you have to create the right environment. You definitely won't get good ideas while watching television, remote control in one hand and popcorn in the other hand. One of the best times to prime your brain to get good ideas is right before going to sleep at night. Instead of watching the late-night news with all those horrible stories—and then spending the whole night running in your sleep after the thief who stole your money—read inspirational and uplifting books. Then close your eyes, let your imagination go wild, make a connection with the universe, and go to sleep.

If you think about your goal before going to sleep, there is a chance that your subconscious mind will work on it while you are sleeping. In the morning, you will be surprised to open your eyes to new ideas, and you may scream, "I found it. I found it. I am a genius! I am a genius!" The fact is, you have always been a genius—you just never learned how to uncover it.

I get most of my good ideas during my early morning walk. It is quiet and peaceful. I let the universe connect with me. Amazingly, I come up with great ideas. Every morning when I go walking, I expect to come back with an idea. It doesn't matter how small, as long as the idea is new. My brain has been trained for it, and lately it has been doing a great job—like coming up with ideas to put in this book. It is very important that you record your daily ideas on your computer or on a piece of paper. If you don't record them, you will forget them.

I believe you are a genius. Just keep digging for those new ideas until one day you hit the gold mine that you have been looking for. Remember, you only need one good idea to be super successful. I believe you are a genius! You just have to uncover it by one idea a day.

SUCCESSFUL PEOPLE
ARE ADDICTED TO LEARNING

All successful people are addicted to learning. They learn until the final day of their lives. They are committed to lifelong learning. If you want to reinvent yourself for success, you must commit yourself to lifelong learning.

Back in 1985, when I started my engineering business, I was working 80 to 100 hours a week. I was married with two boys, and I was willing to do anything to provide a good life for my family. At the same time, financially, I wasn't moving forward in life. I was just paying bills.

Then, one day a successful businessman gave me some great advice. He said, "Paul, success is not the result of hard work alone. In fact, some of the most successful people hardly work. Instead, they read books and attend workshops, seminars, and classes to learn new techniques. They let those techniques do the work for them while they are vacationing in Hawaii." What he said impressed me!

At that time, I committed myself to lifelong learning. I started attending seminars, workshops, and classes. I learned how to deal with people, how to supervise and manage them, and how to bring out the best in them and me. Soon, I felt like people loved to work for me. I was helping them move up in their lives, and they were helping me grow my business. Gradually, I was working less, I was making more money, and I was able to take my family on vacations to Australia, Europe, and Asia.

Will Rogers said, "Even if you're on the right track, you'll get run over if you just sit there." Rogers said it so well! Some people may say, "Paul, I have been successful in the past. If I do what I did in the past, I will be successful again." I have to say that if you do what you did in the past, you may get the same results. The problem is that the world around us keeps changing all the time. The knowledge of the world keeps changing all the time. The bar of excellence keeps rising all the time. If we just sit there and get the same results that we were getting in the past, we may get run over by the world around us.

Rogers was absolutely right! We have to commit ourselves to lifelong learning because everything around us is changing.

SUMMARY

As I mentioned earlier, the taller the building, the deeper the foundation. The taller you want to stand in life, the deeper you have to build your foundation of personal development. There is no way around it. You must commit yourself to lifelong learning to the last day of your life. Lifelong learning will separate you from the pack. Lifelong learning will allow you to reinvent yourself for success, and unleash **THE MILLIONAIRE WITHIN** you. Lifelong learning will take you all the way to the top.

By now, I am sure you are as excited as I am. Let's take a break, then start the final chapter: Pay the Price.

Cardinal Rule #5:

Pay the Price

After the deep foundation has been laid, the construction company starts building the high-rise on top of it—one floor at a time. It is hard work, and the taller the high-rise, the harder the work. They definitely have to Pay the Price and obviously they cannot give up in the middle of the construction process. Just imagine walking through downtown New York and seeing lots of unfinished high-rises. It would be like a ghost town! It would be scary! They would not be usable.

The same thing is true in life. If you want to reinvent yourself for success and unleash **THE MILLIONAIRE WITHIN** you, you have to Pay the Price. You definitely cannot give up. There is no way around it.

I have always known that if I wanted to reach my goal of going "From Stuttering to Professional Speaking," I also had to Pay the Price—and I definitely did—a big price, as you will read in this chapter. I encourage you to make the same commitment.

IT ALL STARTED
WHEN I WAS THREE YEARS OLD

My struggle with stuttering began when I was about three years old. At that time we lived in a small village in north of Iran (just south of Russia). My father owned a small farm, and we led a simple life. I lived with my parents, three sisters, one dog, a few farm animals, and more than one hundred chickens and roosters.

As I was growing up, my stuttering grew up even faster than I did. My parents were very concerned about it, but there was nothing they could do. There was no help available in that small village or in the villages around us. They tried desperately to find a cure for me, but they could not find any. They worried about how I would survive in life, get a job, get married, or have a normal family.

When I was about six, we moved to a small city in the same area so that my three sisters and I could get a formal education. I remember my stuttering got more severe while I was in high school. I knew there was only one way to get out of that miserable life of struggling with my speech—I had to do well in high school so I could get accepted into a university in the capital city of Tehran. I knew I could find the proper treatments in that city.

My hard work paid off. Right after graduating from high school, I got accepted into the top engineering school at the University of Tehran. I was extremely excited about that. Starting in my first semester, I received stuttering therapy. Unfortunately, I later found out they could not offer me any cure. Still, I was determined not to give up and not to lose hope until I reached my dream.

I knew there was only one other way left for me to find a cure for my stuttering—move to the United States. I was confident I would be able to find a cure there. In 1979, I completed my engineering education and I received an invitation to work on my PhD in the state of Ohio. My goals were as follows: to learn the English language, to get my PhD in civil engineering so I could be a college professor, and most importantly, to find a cure for my stuttering. That would be my dream life.

Starting with my first semester in the PhD program, I received speech therapy. I worked myself to the bone with my PhD courses and the stuttering therapy. Now, guess what happened? My stuttering got even worse! I realized that stuttering and learning a new language don't go together very well. In fact, in the first two years my stuttering got so severe that learning sign language seemed to be the best option for me to communicate, and my dreams of finding a cure for my stuttering and becoming a college professor was completely shattered.

After finishing all my PhD courses with straight A's, I didn't see any reason to finish the two-year final project. There was no way I could ever be a college professor. I abandoned my dream and headed west. I found a job in the engineering and construction field.

WHAT IS STUTTERING?

Before I go further, let me explain very briefly what stuttering is:

Stuttering is an incurable speech disorder. About 1% of the population stutters, and approximately 80% of them are male. The reason you may not know many stutterers is that we are expert in hiding our stuttering by changing words, sentences, or by completely avoiding conversation.

At the time of writing this book, the cause of stuttering still is unknown. It is widely believed that in a normal person, the left side of the brain controls the speech muscles and the ability to talk. In the case of stutterers, both hemispheres of the brain try to send nerve impulses. Speech muscles get confused and stuttering happens. Regardless of the causes of stuttering, there is no cure for it, except in very early childhood or in mild cases.

UNCOVERING
THE STATUE OF DAVID

For several years after finishing my PhD courses, I looked for a cure for my stuttering problem without success. In the late 1980s, I read a story that greatly inspired me. The story was about Michelangelo and how he created his masterpiece, The Statue of David—the most famous statue in the world.

As the story goes, there was a big chunk of marble left on the side of the street, and no one was paying any attention to it. It was covered with dirt and trash. One day, as Michelangelo was walking down that street, he saw the figure of David inside that chunk of marble. He took that piece to his shop, grabbed a chisel and a hammer, and started to uncover the masterpiece within.

The story of David and how it was created from a leftover and unwanted chunk of marble covered with dirt and trash inspired me. I was willing to pay any price to reach my goal of overcoming my stuttering and being able to speak in front of people. I just had to uncover the masterpiece within me. I just had to uncover the David inside of me.

I decided to pursue more speech therapy to control my stuttering. All previous attempts had failed, but this time would be different. This time I was inspired by how David had been created. Soon after, I enrolled in three weeks of intensive stuttering therapy, and I went to that stuttering workshop in Washington that I mentioned earlier.

GET OUT OF YOUR COMFORT ZONE

The first week of therapy was very interesting. Our instructors wanted us to build up our self-confidence by stepping out of our comfort zone. We had to go out in public and introduce ourselves as stutterers—something that we had been hiding all of our lives. On top of that, they even wanted us to be humorous about it and laugh at it.

I told them "I will never do that. You should know that stuttering is a speech disorder and is not a funny matter. I am not getting out of my comfort zone; instead, I am getting out of this camp." I found out that the treatment for my stuttering and getting out of my comfort zone was more painful than stuttering itself.

I then said to myself, "If I leave the camp, I will go back to my comfort zone again, and for the rest of my life I will remain like a leftover and unwanted chunk of marble that Michelangelo found on the side of the street." That was not the life that I wanted to live. Even though stepping out of my comfort zone was more painful than stuttering, I decided to stay in the program. Breaking out of my comfort zone in that workshop was the first step toward reaching my goal of overcoming my stuttering.

At the end of the three-week program, I was able to talk with a long prolongation like this: Mmmy nnname iiis PPPaul NNNoor—very basic, and just enough to survive! Even talking like that required a tremendous amount of mental energy, focus, and continuous practice, and there was no guarantee that I could keep my fluency even at that basic level, but I was so excited that at least I had taken the first step out of my comfort zone.

Since my ultimate goal was to be a professional speaker, I decided once again to break out of my comfort zone by joining a Toastmasters public speaking club. Because I was terrified of public speaking, instead of joining them, first I called the president of the club. I told her, "I would love to visit your club, but I am scared of speaking in front of an audience." She said, "Paul, come and visit our club as a guest, and I promise you that no one will ask you any questions. Just sit, relax, and enjoy the program."

I visited that club five times, and every time, I sat by the exit door. I just wanted to make sure that if it got scary, I could run out. Finally I told myself, "If I want to reach my goal of becoming a professional speaker, I have to get out of my comfort zone again and join them. If I stay in my comfort zone I will never grow."

On my sixth visit, I took the first step and I joined that club. A few weeks later, I gave my first speech, and failed badly. I gave more speeches, and I failed more, but I was determined to stay out of my comfort zone, to keep taking risks, and to learn from my failures so that each time I failed, I could build a higher launching pad for my next attempt. After about a year as a member of that club, I was no longer afraid of speaking in front of those people. That club became my new comfort zone.

The comfort zone is an interesting phenomenon. When we move out of our comfort zone, we are just creating a new and larger comfort zone. If we stay in it for a long time, life becomes boring and stagnant—no fun. It will be time to step out of it again. So, one day, I decided to get out of my comfort zone again. Just giving speeches at our club wasn't fun anymore. I decided to give speeches outside of my club.

We all know that it is hard to get out of our comfort zone. The comfort zone is comfortable. That is why we call it the "comfort" zone. We know what to expect. Stepping out of our comfort zone could be scary, but if we stay inside of it, we will confine ourselves to the limited opportunities around us. That is why successful people keep pushing themselves out of their comfort zones. If you want to reinvent yourself for success and unleash **THE MILLIONAIRE WITHIN** you, you must step out of your comfort zone, too.

I was a member of that Toastmasters club for about two years, and I improved a lot. I was able to speak in different places, but because of my stuttering, I wasn't able to reach my dream life of becoming a professional speaker. I wasn't able to fully uncover the David inside of me. I came to the painful conclusion that my stuttering and professional speaking do not go together very well. Sadly, I left that Toastmasters club, and I abandoned the David project. Once again, my dream had been shattered.

THE SECOND CHANCE

As I mentioned earlier, while I was at the very peak of success with my home building business, I became entangled in an unfortunate and destructive divorce. Because of the stress that I was under, my stuttering was at its worst.

When I was down at the lowest point of my life, I remembered what Charles Darwin wrote: "It is not the strongest of the species that survives, nor the most intelligent that survives. It is the one that is the most adaptable to change." He wrote it many years ago, but it seemed as if he had written it specifically for me.

I quickly realized that the secret to my survival would be to accept the changes in my life and move forward toward a better future. I thought that was my last chance to go "From Stuttering to Professional Speaking." I then decided to complete the abandoned project of uncovering the David inside of me that I had started about fifteen years earlier.

This time I was willing to pay any price—I mean any price, and I did.

1. I worked religiously on my stuttering reduction techniques. I used some of the techniques that I had learned in the past, and I came up with a few techniques of my own. I practiced about four hours every day.

2. I rejoined Toastmasters. At one point, I was a member of four clubs simultaneously so that I could practice my speeches in front of four different audiences.

3. I started reading motivational and inspirational books. I read one book per week. As I was reading, I was becoming even more motivated and inspired to reach my goals.

4. I hired an international keynote speaker and a world champion of public speaking to coach me.

5. I hired a professional actor who was also a college professor teaching public speaking and acting. He helped me with pronunciation, articulation, and the acting part of public speaking.

I then spoke at schools, colleges, universities, churches, prisons, hospitals, Rotary Clubs, Lions Clubs, and any group willing to listen to me. I practiced, and I failed. I practiced more, and I failed more. I practiced even more, and I failed even more. This time, I refused to give up. This time, I refused to go back to my comfort zone. This time, I refused to remain as a leftover chunk of marble on the side of the street.

All of that hard work paid off. As I mentioned earlier, two years later, I was the keynote speaker at a convention in California. Since then I have spoken at numerous places including Fortune 500 companies. How is that for a change? One of the reasons why I was able to reach my goal in spite of all of the odds being against me was that I got out of my comfort zone, I Paid the Price, and I did not give up.

Are you willing to Pay the Price, too?

If you want to reinvent yourself for success and

unleash **THE MILLIONAIRE WITHIN** you, you must Pay the Price.

Remember, you are the only one who can change yourself.

You are the only one who can uncover the masterpiece within you.

You are the only one who can uncover the David inside of you.

Let today be the start of a new beginning in your life.

EXPECT FAILURE IN YOUR JOURNEY

A few months after graduating from the stuttering workshop, I lost my fluency and had to go back to the same workshop three more summers. The last two times, I worked as an assistant therapist helping other stutterers who had come from around the world. I thought the best way to master any skill would be to teach it. In order for me to teach other stutterers, I had to be a good role model. To be that, I intensely practiced all the stuttering therapy techniques.

I don't want to sound negative and talk about

failures, but the fact is that when you step out of your comfort zone to reinvent yourself for success, failure will be part of your journey. Even after I had attended the same workshop four times, there was one occasion when I gave a presentation to a gathering and I couldn't control my stuttering. My fluency almost went back to square one. I went home, and I collapsed in bed. I felt like a man who had been hit by a freight train.

Then an inner voice said, "Paul, you have tried for many years. One day you will have to accept the fact that stuttering and public speaking don't go together very well. One day you will have to accept the fact that you were not born to be a speaker. Don't make a fool of yourself in front of other people. Stop public speaking and go back to your comfort zone—the same life you had before."

Then another voice said, "Paul, don't quit! You have come too far to quit. Yes, you failed tonight, but you came this far because you had failed so many times before, and you learned from your failures. Tonight's failure was big, but it also means that you will learn a big lesson from it. Don't quit Paul! Don't quit!"

The first voice immediately came back and said, "Paul, just listen to me. Public speaking is not for you. Don't make a fool of yourself. Stop public speaking, and go back to the life you had before. Go back to your comfort zone."

I screamed, "Stop! Stop! I am not going to listen to you."

I lectured myself, "If I listen to the negative voice, I will be feeding it, and it will become stronger, and stronger, and stronger. Eventually, it will be so strong that it will push me back into my comfort zone, and for the rest of my life, I will remain like a leftover chunk of marble. Instead, I will listen to the positive voice. By listening to the positive voice, I will feed it and it will become stronger, and stronger, and stronger. Eventually, I will make this voice so strong that it will push my masterpiece out of my marble."

When you step out of your comfort zone to reach your goals and live your dream life, failures will be part of the journey. My question to you is: Which voice are you going to listen to? Will you be defeated by your failures, or will you take advantage of them and turn them into a strong positive force to carve your David out of your marble? The choice is yours.

THOMAS EDISON NEVER GAVE UP

A good example of a successful person who never gave up is Thomas Edison. It has been said that he tried thousands of times to invent the light bulb. Even after all of those trials, he said, "I have not failed. I've just found another way that won't work."

When it comes to handling failures, Thomas Edison's is inspiring. On December 9, 1914, Edison Industries burned to the ground. He lost about two million dollars—a huge fortune in those days. Most of his work went up in flames.

At that time, he was sixty-seven years old. It seemed as if he had no future left. Instead, Edison said, "There is great value in disaster. All our mistakes are burned up. Thank God we can start fresh." About three weeks after that fire, his company delivered the first phonograph! Wow! Thomas Edison, Walt Disney, and Abraham Lincoln all failed many times. They reached the top because they Paid the Price, and they did not give up.

Are you willing to Pay the Price, too?

If you want to reinvent yourself for success and unleash **THE MILLIONAIRE WITHIN** you, you must Pay the Price.

LAUGH AT YOUR FAILURES

Humor lifts the pressure off our shoulders. It creates a better environment in which we can overcome our challenges. Learn to laugh at your failures.

When I first joined Toastmasters, because of my struggle with stuttering, the twenty members of that club were extremely kind to me. As soon as they heard my stuttering, they paid special attention to me and took me under their wing. They were hoping that one day I would be able to stand on my feet and speak in front of people.

In the first year, I worked very hard and I even won the speech contest at our club. They could not believe it. They had no idea that my stuttering actually was giving me a great advantage in public speaking! I kept it a secret, and I never told them anything about it. You see, at that time my stuttering was so bad that for a five- to seven-minute speech, I only had to write twenty seconds of speech material. By the time I had added my stuttering, it would easily be more than seven minutes.

When I joke about my stuttering, I am letting everybody know that I am not afraid of it. I am putting everybody at ease, including me, and that paves the road to recovery. I believe it is true in all aspects of life. Not only that, it is always better to laugh with the audience than be laughed at by them.

BEING IN PRISON GAVE ME THE BOOST

Early in my speaking career, a local prison invited me to give a presentation to about one hundred prisoners who were about to be released. They had gone through intense training and were ready to re-enter the outside world. Before I spoke, the supervisor of the facility told me, "Paul, they are not here to listen to your presentation. They are here because they are told to be here. If they show disrespect, don't take it personally."

I said, "Don't worry. I was in the rough construction business for many years. I know how to handle the situation. Leave it to me."

I started the program at 8:00 p.m. It was a one-hour presentation. I basically covered the Five Cardinal Rules in this book. When I ended my presentation, all one hundred prisoners gave me a standing ovation, and some lined up to shake hands with me. They thanked me for giving them a new direction in life. I could see their hope for a better future was shining in their eyes, and the joy of being able to inspire and help them was bubbling inside of me. I could hardly sleep that night.

I felt as if finally I was able to make something good out of my miserable life of severe stuttering. I was on cloud nine. I knew I was on to something. At that point, there was no force in the world that could have stopped me. I became like an avalanche, gaining momentum as I was moving forward, demolishing any remaining obstacles, resistance, and fear that were left on my path toward completely uncovering the David inside of me. It was an unforgettable night. The reason I was able to do well that night was that I got out of my comfort zone, I

Paid the Price, and I did not give up.

Are you willing to Pay the Price, too?

If you want to reinvent yourself for success and unleash **THE MILLIONAIRE WITHIN** you, you must Pay the Price.

I PAID THE PRICE
TO WRITE THIS BOOK

I have never written a book before. I am not a professional writer. As I said earlier, English is my second language. I practically learned it at the age of 25 when I moved to the United States.

In order to write this book, I became an avid reader. I read one book per week, summarized it, and then typed the summary. I thought this would be the best way to become a writer.

Since I wanted my book to be inspirational and educational, I mainly read books by great authors who inspired me. I wanted to do the same for others: inspire and educate them through my writing. Slowly, I learned to write, and gradually I began writing this book—one page at a time.

After writing each section, I would deliver a speech on that topic to various Toastmasters, Rotary, and Lions Clubs. I wanted to test the material and get feedback from live audiences. After each presentation, I would polish my speech before presenting it to the next group. Sometimes, I would give the same presentation to different groups on the same day. This way, I was getting feedback for my book, practicing my stuttering therapy techniques, and improving my public speaking skills —all at the same time. Sometimes I had to drive more than an hour to practice in front of a new group or give a free speech at a Rotary Club, just to get feedback so I could polish that part of the book.

I was able to write this book because, I got out of my comfort zone, I Paid the Price, and I did not give up.

Are you willing to Pay the Price, too?

If you want to reinvent yourself for success and unleash **THE MILLIONAIRE WITHIN** you, you must Pay the Price, too.

A GREAT LESSON FROM A FARMER

One day a farmer gave a great life lesson to his son. He took a small seed and planted it under a few inches of dirt. He then said, "Son, the dirt above that seed is much heavier than the weight of the seed. The seed has absolutely no chance to get out of that hole. But the seed has life in it. If we plant the seed in the fertile soil and water it, a plant will grow out of it, and the plant will grow taller and stronger every day, and it will eventually burst through the heavy weight of the dirt above it. That small seed could have the potential to become a magnificent tree, providing shade and fresh oxygen for everybody."

Wow! What a great life lesson! The same thing is true in life. We all have seeds of greatness inside of us. We were born with them. If you plant them in fertile and positive environments, you will get stronger every day, and you will eventually burst through the heavy pressure above and around you.

I believe the Five Cardinal Rules that I discussed in this book will create the right environment for you to reinvent yourself for success and unleash **THE MILLIONAIRE WITHIN** you.

129

THE END

Congratulations! You have completed all Five Cardinal Rules. I recommend that you read this book again. Go to the first page, read, and most importantly, take action as you read. Master each Cardinal Rule before you go to the next one, and repeat the process as many times as needed.

As I said at the beginning of this book, life has so many ups and downs. Sometimes you have to close an old chapter and start a new one. When that happens, you have two options: either to put your failures, setbacks, and all those painful memories right in front of you like a wall and let it stop you from moving forward, or to use these Five Cardinal Rules to reinvent yourself for success and unleash **THE MILLIONAIRE WITHIN** you. I strongly recommend that you choose the second option—because you deserve to be successful.

Paul
PaulNoor.com

Revised: April 21, 2017

ABOUT THE AUTHOR

Paul Noor is an Author, Speaker, and Corporate Trainer. He has spoken at numerous organizations, including Fortune-500 companies.

Paul has traveled around the globe and he would love to be the speaker at your next EVENT—in any corner of the World.

Invite Paul Noor to speak at your next conference or convention. Also invite him to present a seminar at your workplace to train your team. His presentations are Inspirational, Educational, and Entertaining.

www.PaulNoor.com

Pay the Price